THE MEDIEVAL MONASTERY

First published 1958
Ninth impression 1973

ISBN 0 582 20372 4

Printed in Hong Kong by
Peninsula Press Ltd

THEN AND THERE FILMSTRIPS
are now available

The Medieval World
Three full-colour, double frame filmstrips,
in a boxed set

Filmstrip 1
Royalty; Knights, Castles, Tournaments;
Religious Life

Filmstrip 2
Country Life; Sports and Pastimes

Filmstrip 3
Town Life; Home Life; Travel

Write to Longman for details or for one set
on approval

LONGMAN GROUP LIMITED
London

*Associated companies, branches and representatives
throughout the world*

© Marjorie Reeves 1958

First published 1958
Ninth impression 1973

ISBN 0 582 20372 4

*Printed in Hong Kong by
Peninsula Press Ltd*

THEN AND THERE FILMSTRIPS
are now available

The Medieval World
Three full-colour, double frame filmstrips, in a boxed set

Filmstrip 1
Royalty; Knights, Castles, Tournaments; Religious Life

Filmstrip 2
Country Life; Sports and Pastimes

Filmstrip 3
Town Life; Home Life; Travel

Write to Longman for details or for one set on approval

THEN AND THERE SERIES
GENERAL EDITOR
MARJORIE REEVES, M.A., Ph.D.

The Medieval Monastery

MARJORIE REEVES, M.A. Ph.D.

Illustrated from contemporary sources by

H. C. MCBEATH

LONGMAN

To my nephew Anthony Sheppard

Acknowledgments

We are indebted to the following for permission to quote copyright material: Messrs. A. & C. Black Ltd. for St. Ailred's Prayer from *The Pastoral Prayer of St. Ailred*, translated by 'A Religious of C.S.M.V.'; Messrs. Chatto & Windus Ltd. for extracts from Gasquet's translation of *St. Benedict's Rule* (*The King's Classics*); and Messrs. Thomas Nelson & Sons Ltd. for extracts from *The Monastic Constitutions of Lanfranc*, translated by D. Knowles, and *Jocelyn of Brakelond's Chronicle*, translated by H. Buter.

For permission to include drawings based on copyright material we are indebted to the following: Macmillan & Co. Ltd. – pages 3 and 18 from *Green: Short History of the English People Vol. 1*; Cambridge University Press – pages 20 and 53 from *Hamilton Thompson: English Monasteries*; the Controller of H.M.S.O. – page 23 based on the more detailed plan published by the Ministry of Works; George Philip & Son, Ltd. – pages 41 and 50 from *Social & Economic Histories Book 2*; Methuen & Co. Ltd. – page 57 adapted from *Gasquet: English Monastic Life*; Dean and Chapter of Winchester – pages 69 and 70 (initial); British Museum – page 73; National Gallery of Art, Washington – page 83.

CONTENTS

TO THE READER

MONKS and monasteries seem, perhaps, rather far away from the lives most of us live today, although there are still many people who follow the monastic life in joy and usefulness. Perhaps you know some of them. It is important to try and understand what they really think and feel about this special life of theirs. This book is about monks who lived about seven hundred years ago. They wrote much about their life and often drew pictures too. I have tried to let them speak for themselves in words and drawings, so that you can get a true idea of what it was like to live in a monastery in the twelfth century. You will find out more about these words and pictures by reading pages 81–83. You will also find a useful map on page 87.

By studying what people said in word and picture about themselves, you will come to feel at home in one 'patch' of the history of the past and really live with one group of people as they thought and worked. And gradually you will be able to fill in more patches of history.

The THEN AND THERE Series now has three books with the word MEDIEVAL in the title: THE MEDIEVAL VILLAGE, THE MEDIEVAL TOWN and THE MEDIEVAL MONASTERY. Have you yet discovered what the word *Medieval* means? It comes from two Latin words *Medium Aevum*, meaning the Middle Age. The monks, of course, wrote Latin and therefore used these words, but they did not call their own time the middle age—to them it was the latest age. But later on, historians, looking back over the centuries between about 800 and 1500, thought of them as coming between ancient times and their own modern times. So they called them the *Medium Aevum*, the Middle or Medieval Age.

AILRED COMES TO RIEVAULX

THE court of King David of Scotland about eight hundred years ago was an exciting place for a young man. There were knights and huntsmen, grave *counsellors*[1] and churchmen; there were messengers and strangers coming and going; there was fighting to be done and, when fighting was over, there was feasting. The young man Ailred was a favourite with the king and with all his courtiers, for he was sweet-tempered and sweet-tongued, doing no man any wrong and serving his king faithfully. King David made him chief *steward*, and so, when the great hall was filled with folk ready to eat and drink their fill, he would stand beside the king serving the dishes. Then the king would notice how, in the midst of the noise, he would sometimes stand in a dream, dividing the food to others but eating none himself. His thoughts were far away—beyond the crackle and blaze of the great fire, beyond the bustle and clatter of dishes, beyond the merry talk and the harpist's song. In his mind's eye he saw another world of holiness and stillness, where men served God first of all, and this was the world in which he longed to be. But he told no one.

One day in the year 1134 Ailred rode south from Scotland on the great road to York. Here he heard about 'the White Monks'. He was told that these monks had come to England two years before and settled like a flock of white seagulls by a lonely stream. He was told that these holy men of God shone like snow in their purity. When he heard this, he exclaimed: "Where, oh where is the way to

1 You will find words printed like *this* in the glossary on pages 88–90.

these angelic men?" "They are close at hand," was the reply, "You can see them before the sun sets." So Ailred jumped on his horse again and rode on until he found the monks at a place called Rievaulx.[1] He came to the edge of a hill and there below him saw this green valley with steep hills on either side:

The River Rie rushed and tumbled down it with a gentle murmur of soft sound, while all around the trees rustled and sang together. As Ailred rode quietly through the valley he seemed to hear music all round him. He came to some rough huts which the monks had built for themselves. At the gate Ailred was met by the gatekeeper and two other monks. They talked to him of holy things, and as they talked he wept for his sins and longed to stay there.

[1] Pronounced 'Reevo'; it means the valley of the River Rie.

But that night he went away to a nearby castle belonging to a knight named Walter Espec. Perhaps Ailred and Walter talked about which was best—the knight's life of fighting or the monk's life of praying.

In the morning Ailred had still not made up his mind. He started home for Scotland, but as he rode along the edge of the hill above the *monastery*, he came to a path leading down to it. He stopped and asked one of his servants: "Shall we go down again and see this holy place?" If the servant had answered 'No,' he would have ridden on home; but the servant said 'Yes,' so they went down the path. A crowd of monks flocked out to meet them. Once again Ailred felt a fierce longing to join them. And now his mind was made up. He would never go back to King David and his court in Scotland; he would stay and be a monk at Rievaulx!

Here is a procession of monks such as Ailred might have seen:

ST. BENEDICT AND HIS RULE FOR MONKS

MANY hundreds of years before Ailred, there had lived another man who longed to get away from the noise of many people. His name was Benedict and he lived in Italy. It was a time of wars and sudden alarms. Tribes of fierce men were invading Italy. They had overthrown the Roman Emperor and set up their own kings, but no one could guess what would happen next and no one felt safe.

Benedict was sent to school in Rome, but there he was horrified at the evil way men lived. So he ran away into the mountains and there he found a new way to escape from fear and evil. His way was to forget about danger and live in some quiet place where he would try to please God alone. If the fierce invaders came, he would not try to fight them with spears and swords, but instead would try to make them live at peace under God. For some time Benedict lived in a cave high up on the mountain of Subiaco, thinking out his plan. Then friends and followers gathered round him and built the first house or monastery of the monks of Benedict. Soon many others were wanting to join and more

St. Benedict praying outside
his cave

4

monasteries (or *abbeys*) were built, especially in lonely places.

Here is a much later picture of the most famous of the Benedictine abbeys—Monte Cassino, where St. Benedict finally went to live, and where he died in the year 543:

It stands on the top of a mountain. Far down below, Benedict must often have seen armies marching to cruel battle or burning towns, but they never harmed the holy men of God. So Benedict's monasteries became little islands of peace in the midst of war. Indeed, one wild and fierce king named Totila, who came to visit Benedict, listened without getting angry while the saint commanded him not to be so cruel.

St. Benedict wrote a set of rules for his monks. He called it a very little rule for beginners, because he wanted his monasteries to be schools for the service of God, and so the rules must not be too difficult at the beginning. We now call it St. Benedict's Rule (with a capital R).

He said the monks must learn to serve God in three ways. First, they were to sing His praises and pray in the chapel at least eight times a day, starting so early that it was still dark, and finishing just before they went to bed. So at intervals all through the day the Work of God, as they called it, went on—praise and homage to the real King of the monastery.

The second kind of service was what we should call ordinary work. Part of it was work with the hands—digging in the fields, baking and cooking, washing and cleaning. Part of it was reading the Bible and thinking about the Word of God.

The third way in which the monks served God was by self-discipline, that is, by being ready to give up doing what they wanted, if it was against the Rule. St. Benedict allowed his monks only one or two meals a day and no meat at any meal; he made them get up and go to bed at set times, and he made very strict rules about silence. But he did see that his monks had enough to eat and drink, enough time to sleep, and some times when they could talk to each other. So the discipline was not too hard. Perhaps the hardest things to learn were to obey cheerfully and not to quarrel with the other monks.

St. Benedict's Rule says what is to happen when a man knocks at the gate of the monastery asking to become a monk. They must not let him in too easily. The monks must keep him waiting four or five days to see if he can be patient. After that he can become a *novice* or learner. The teacher of the novices must tell him all about the monk's life and after two months must read the whole Rule to him and say: "See the law under which you wish to live. If you can keep it, enter upon the life; if you cannot, you are free to go." If the novice says the Rule is not too hard and he wants to stay, he must go on learning for a whole year. Then he is made a proper monk.

All the monks meet together and in front of them the novice makes his promises (or *vows*) to keep the Rule and be obedient. Then he gives to the monastery all his money and other possessions, even his clothes. From now on he will have nothing of his own but will share in all that the monastery has.

He now puts on the special dress of the monks, which is called a *habit*. The picture above shows a new monk receiving the habit. St. Benedict said the habit must be made of coarse, hard-wearing stuff, and, as it was usually dark in colour, his monks came to be called the Black Monks. This picture shows you what their habit was like.

The head of the whole monastery was called the *Abbot*. St. Benedict said that he was to be the father of all the monks. Like a shepherd

A Benedictine Abbot

guarding his sheep, he was to watch over his flock. It was the monks' duty to obey him, and it was the Abbot's duty not to command anything wrong or too difficult. If a monk disobeyed, the Abbot must rebuke him. If he went on disobeying he must be punished; but, said St. Benedict, the Abbot must try all ways to make him good before he punished him severely. Every day the Abbot called all the monks together in a council or *chapter*, as it was called, to settle all the business of the monastery. When the Abbot died, the monks met together in their chapter to choose the wisest of them all to be their new abbot.

St. Benedict wanted each of his monasteries to be a real family of monks, a good family in which all the members helped each other. He told them to speak politely to each other and never take sides in quarrels. One small way in which he told them they could help each other was in getting up punctually in the morning. It was dark and often cold when they had to arise, and St. Benedict said that the good risers should stir up the sleepy-heads who liked to lie in bed. Would this be a good idea in your family?

THE WHITE MONKS

MANY people wanted to become Black Monks and join one of St. Benedict's families. So Benedictine monasteries were built in many places in Italy, Germany and France. They came to England and built splendid monasteries here too. Find out, if you can, if there is a Benedictine monastery anywhere near your home or school.

But, as time went on, Benedictine monks began to get lazy and rich. They did not keep the Rule so well and lived too comfortably. So several men who wanted to serve God by living a stricter life started new companies of monks who went back to St. Benedict's first Rule. One small company started in the woods in a lonely part of Burgundy (in France). They chose the place because the bushes all round were so thick that visitors could not get through to disturb them. They made their habits out of grey-white sheep's wool, so they were called White Monks. This is what they looked like.

Their life was so strict and hard that not many people could stand it. The little company got smaller and smaller and was nearly giving up altogether when one day, in front of the monastery gate, there stood a splendid young man with rosy cheeks and fair hair, knocking and asking to become a White Monk. And with him were thirty other young men!

This young man was called Bernard. He was well-born, rich and handsome, but he counted the service of God more precious than anything else. He had a wonderful way of making everyone around him enthusiastic—as if he carried a lighted candle in his hand from which he could light up everyone he met. So when he rode off to be a monk all these other young men were eager to do the same. Bernard and his friends all joined the White Monks at their monastery at Citeaux.[1]

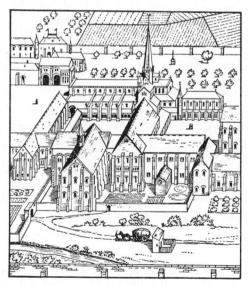

Citeaux with many later buildings.

[1] Pronounced ' Seeto '.

Soon many other young men were going there, for Bernard preached and wrote to many people and his words were like sparks flying round to catch men's souls on fire. So the White Monks of Citeaux became famous. People called them Cistercians, after their house at Citeaux, and soon there were Cistercian monasteries all over Europe.

Here is a picture which someone many years later drew of Bernard, holding a model of the Abbey Church at Citeaux.

Before long some adventurous Yorkshiremen travelled across the sea to visit Bernard. Perhaps they told him about the lonely

dales of Yorkshire, for the Cistercian monks liked quiet places to live in, far away from the hustle and bustle of towns. Bernard promised to send some of his monks to England, and so, in the year 1131, a band of White Monks set out from Burgundy and walked all the way to Yorkshire (except when they crossed the Channel in a boat). When they reached the city of York they rested in a house of Black Monks, called St. Mary's Abbey. But they would not stop in the noisy town, so on they went for another thirty miles, until at last they came to the wild and lovely dale of the River Rie. There they stayed, and there Ailred found them at Rievaulx about two years later.

THE BUILDING OF RIEVAULX

AT FIRST there was only an abbot, named William, and twelve monks. It was a hard struggle to live, for they had to do all the work with their own hands. Walter Espec (the knight in whose castle Ailred stayed) gave them a small piece of land, and here they built rough wooden huts for themselves and started to grow some food. Walter Espec also let them cut firewood in his forest, and how glad they were in the first cold winters! For they had little to eat and their poor little huts would not keep out the bitter winds. But they would not spend any time making themselves comfortable, for they were all eager to start building their church.

Walter Espec must have been a jolly old knight. Ailred tells us that he was very tall, with black hair (even when he was old), long beard, large bright eyes, and a voice as loud as a trumpet. He had been a great fighter when he was young, but now this old warrior became a true friend of the White Monks. When they had toiled hard for some time on their little piece of land he gave them a much better piece where they could really start building in earnest.

By this time many more monks had joined—Ailred was one of them—and there were plenty of eager hands to build. And what a lot there was to do! As the valley was narrow, with steep sides, they had first to cut away the steep bank and make a terrace, in order to get a large flat place on which to build the church. Monks always liked to have their church facing towards the sunrise in the east, but at Rievaulx there was not room for it in this way. So they planned the church facing nearly south. Down below it, on another terrace, they planned the rest of the monastery according to the usual Cistercian pattern.

Next, they had to find stone for building, and here they were lucky, for only a quarter of a mile away, close to the river bank at a place called Penny Rise, they found dark brown sandstone which was easy to cut. You can still see today where they quarried the stone and you can still see the clever way in which they got the stone to the terrace. To drag stone even a quarter of a mile is slow and heavy work, so they dammed up the river and cut a canal to bring the water close to the terrace. Then they made a raft and floated all the stones along the canal. Here is a plan showing all these things:

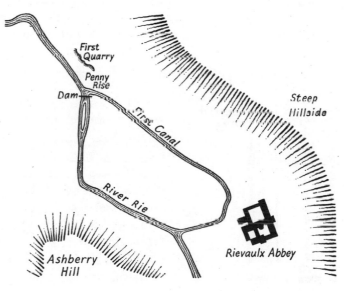

And here are two monks carrying a stone on a tray.

The first thing to build was the church. Bernard had made a strict rule for the Cistercians that all their churches were to be very plain, not decorated with gold or silver or paint. So the monks of Rievaulx made a plain but dignified church in the shape of a cross, with round-headed windows and round pillars. The end where the altar stood was called the *presbytery*, the two arms of the cross were the *transepts*, and the long part was the *nave*. The monks sat in the part called the monks' choir, and the lay brothers (about whom I shall be telling you later) sat in the part called the lay brothers' choir. The monks sat in wooden seats called *stalls*, arranged in two rows facing each other on either side of the choir. In the middle was a large *lectern* or reading desk. The two choirs were separated by two screens called the *pulpitum* and the *rood-screen*. Now find all these different parts on the plan.

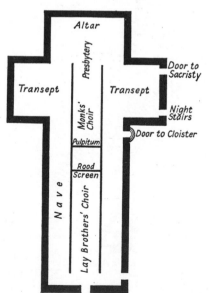

Over the centre of the church they built a *belfry* with a
big bell. You will soon discover why this big bell was so
important. I cannot show you a picture of what the church
looked like when it was finished, for today it is all in ruins.
But here is another Cistercian church:

Below the church the monks built their *cloister*. This
was really their home: here they got ready to meet God
in the church, and here, when they came out of church,
they sat to read or to think. So they liked to put it on the
sunny side of the church, sheltered from the cold winds.

It had four covered walks arranged in a square. In this picture of a cloister you can see all four walks and open space in the middle:

This picture of another cloister will give you an idea of what the Rievaulx cloister may have looked like:

All the monks had their own special seats in the cloister. In the walk next to the church (usually called the north walk, although at Rievaulx it was not really on the north side of the cloister), sat the oldest monks, with the Abbot next to the steps leading up to the church. They probably had wooden desks for writing, and in one corner there was a cupboard for books. In the east walk sat the novices with the *novice-master*, in the west walk sat the young monks and lay brothers, while the south walk was kept as a passage.

Next to the church on the east side of the cloister, the monks built a *chapter-house* for their daily meetings. This was a big room with rows of slender pillars to hold up the roof, which probably looked like this:

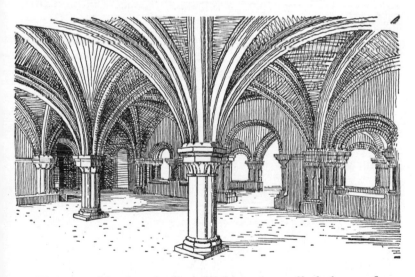

Next to this they built a little room called the *parlour*. We today think of a parlour as a sitting-room, but the monks who first invented the word meant a speaking-room. The first Cistercian monks were mostly French

and used a French word 'parler' 'to speak.' So the parlour
was the only room where monks could speak to each other
or to visitors; everywhere else they had to keep silence.
Next to the parlour they built a Treasury and then a room
which they must have longed for during those first cold
winters—a warming-room! This had a large fireplace and
a great chimney, and here, from the beginning of November to the end of March, there was a cheerful fire. Then
the cold monks, sitting in the cloisters with their teeth
chattering, would be allowed sometimes to go in and warm
themselves. But they were not allowed to stay long and
make themselves cosy.

Now at last the monks were ready to build themselves a
proper dormitory (or *dorter*) to sleep in! I wonder if all
this time they had been sleeping in those wretched little
huts. For the dorter they made one great, long room
which extended right over the chapter-house, parlour and
warming-room. It was 200 feet long and divided by partitions into cubicles. Here they are, hard at work building it:

At the end nearest the church, there was a stone staircase going straight down into the church. It was called the night stairs, and you will soon be finding out what this was for. Another staircase, called the day stairs, went down into the cloister.

In the dorter all the monks slept together. Each one had a pillow and a blanket, but no mattress, only a mat. The younger monks were placed between the older ones. Can you guess why they were arranged like this? Besides the beds, there was very little furniture in the dormitory—no mirrors or chests or drawers or wardrobes. Monks did not use these things, for they had few clothes and no other possessions of their own. The walls were bare, except perhaps for a crucifix hanging at one end.

On the side of the cloister opposite the church they built the *refectory* (or *frater*)—the monks' dining-room. At the door there was a row of basins for washing hands and a cupboard for towels. The refectory was a long room with long, narrow tables and benches. At the end was the high table with a chair for the Abbot or the *Prior* (who was next in command) and by it was a bell which was rung at the beginning and end of every meal as a signal for saying grace. Built in one wall there was a pulpit where the Reader stood, for there was no talking at meals; instead, one of the monks read aloud from the Bible. The pulpit probably looked like this:

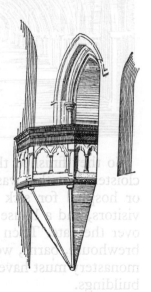

The kitchen was next door to the refectory, with a window or hatch for passing dishes through.

Finally, in the west side of the cloister, the monks built a long, narrow store-house for all their food, etc., called the *cellarium*, which looked like this:

So they finished the buildings on all four sides of the cloister. But this was not all. They needed an *infirmary* or hospital for sick and old monks, a guest-house for visitors, and a house where the porter could keep watch over the gate. Then they had to build a bakehouse and brewhouse, barns, workshops, and a mill. In the end the monastery must have looked like a small town with all its buildings.

Here is a plan of Rievaulx in Ailred's time:

1 Steps up to Church
2 Cupboard for books
3 Night Stairs to Dormitory
4 Day Stairs to Dormitory

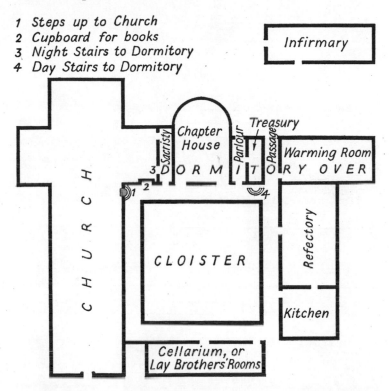

In all this hard work of quarrying, building, making furniture, etc., the monks must have been greatly helped by the lay brothers. But one of the puzzles at Rievaulx is that we cannot be sure where the lay brothers slept and ate their meals. In Cistercian houses their refectory was usually on the other side of the kitchen from the monks' refectory, and their dorter was over the storehouse on the west side of the cloister, with their own staircase down into the nave of the church. At Rievaulx there is no sign of

Rievaulx today.

these rooms. Perhaps one day, when more of the ruins have been *excavated*, we shall find the answer to this puzzle, for they probably did live over the cellarium.

It was most important to the monks to have a good water-supply, and this they found quite easy because there were many streams flowing down the hillside. So they built a large stone tank to collect water and then laid lead pipes to carry the water to where it was needed.

All this building went on for many years and by the time it was finished there were so many monks at Rievaulx that they had to start enlarging the church. By that time Ailred was the Abbot, and he planned a lot of new buildings himself. How we should like to see all those buildings standing white and clean as when they were new! But today Rievaulx is all in ruins, with ivy growing over it and owls hooting through the broken arches. You can see from the picture opposite what these ruins look like today, and here is a plan to help you recognize the different parts. Compare it with the plan on page 21, and the picture on page 48.

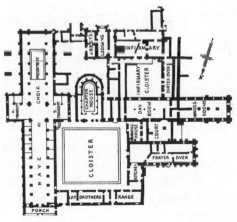

HOW AILRED LIVED AT RIEVAULX

WHEN Ailred decided to be a monk he divided his money and possessions among his friends and servants and sent them all away, except the one who had told him to go to the monastery. Then he waited, very impatiently, for four days in the guest-house. Why did St. Benedict's Rule require this waiting period? While Ailred was in the guest-house, a fire broke out and the monks were pleased with his quickness in jumping up instantly and putting out the flames with a jug of beer. At last he was brought before all the monks, seated together in their chapter. When they asked him why he wished to be a monk, he answered so humbly and sweetly that they all loved him. So they received him as a novice.

He put on the novice's habit and began to learn how to be a monk. His teacher or novice-master was named Simon. Many years later, when Ailred was dead and Simon an old, old man, he talked to some monks about Ailred when he was a young novice. He said he was never gloomy or sad, even when made to do hard things, but always full of joy, like a lamb skipping about among the sheep. And remember, it was hard to be a novice—to sleep on bare boards when you were used to a mattress, to get up in the dark and cold when you wanted to lie snug and warm, to eat bread and vegetables when you were longing for some roast meat, to keep silence when you loved talking! All these and many other hard things Ailred learnt to do joyfully.

The novices sat together in the cloister. There they learnt what the Rule of St. Benedict meant, how to read and write, and how to sing the psalms and other parts of the church services from memory. At the end of two months, and again after six, the whole Rule was read to them and they were asked if they wanted to go on becoming monks. Ailred never hesitated at all but always said 'Yes.' At the end of a year he made his full vows or promises and so he became a full monk. When he put on the white habit his rosy cheeks and bright face made the other monks think of King David in the Bible. Now he found that life was even busier and harder, but still he was merry.

The monks had a very strict time-table: let us find out how they lived in winter and summer.

In winter-time the bell sounded in the dark, cold night about 2 A.M. I wonder how the monk who had the duty of ringing it knew the right hour, for he had no clock or watch. If he overslept, he had to say some extra prayers for punishment (*penance* it was called). The monks got up from their mats in the dark dorter, roused up the sleepy-heads, and went in pro-cession down the night stairs to the church to sing the service called *Vigils*. The church was like a great pool of darkness with a few little flickering lights. Each monk knelt in his own place in the choir, the Abbot farthest from the high altar and the youngest monk nearest to it.

Then, singing from memory in the gloom, they began the solemn chanting of psalms. Sometimes the Abbot went round with a lantern to make sure that no one had fallen asleep, but the grave, mysterious singing went steadily on.

After this night service the monks spent some time praying in church or reading in the cloisters by the light of flickering lamps. Although they wore warm boots, it must have been very cold as they waited for the bell to ring again. (In the coldest part of the year after Christmas, they were allowed to warm themselves by the fire in the warming-room.) When sunrise was near, the bell rang and they all went back to the church to sing the joyful service called *Matins* or *Lauds*, because they praised Christ, their rising sun, singing a sunrise hymn which began *Jam lucis orto sidere* (in English, "The star of morn has risen"). Here are the monks singing one of the services:

Soon after this, at about 6 A.M., they sang the first service of the day, called *Prime*. Immediately after, one of the monks celebrated High Mass at the high altar. Then came the next service called *Tierce*, and after this all the monks went to the chapter-house for their daily meeting.

The Abbot sat solemnly in his high seat and everyone else had his own seat in order, from the oldest down to the newest member of the company. First the Abbot read the names of the special saints for the day and they all said prayers for faithful monks who had died in the monastery. Then a chapter from St. Benedict's Rule was read aloud: this was why the whole meeting was called a chapter. Sometimes the Abbot also preached a sermon. Then they turned to practical business. Each monk was told what work he had to do that day. He was expected to do it without grumbling, but if he wanted to make an excuse he had to do it at once in the chapter, or not at all.

Finally, all the novices went out and then the monks who had done wrong were punished. Often a monk who knew he had done his work badly, or talked when he should have been silent, or fallen asleep during Vigils, confessed his fault and asked pardon. But some were too proud to do this, so their wrong-doings had to be told by other monks before the whole chapter. Then the Abbot would say how they were punished—by living on bread and water for several days, or by eating meals alone, or by being sent down to the lowest place, or even by being whipped. If a monk was whipped, the rest sat with bowed and covered heads to show how sorry they were. Now and again a really bad monk was imprisoned in a little stone cell, or even expelled from the monastery. Whatever happened in the chapter, everyone had to keep silent about it after they had left the chapter-house.

Here is a picture of some monks meeting in their chapter (though not at Rievaulx):

After the chapter meeting everyone went to work, praising God with their hands in the kitchen or workshop or fields. The Prior sat in the parlour and directed the work, giving the monks the tools they needed. The next part of this book will tell you more about their work. At noon came the next service, *Sext*. If the monks were away in the fields when the abbey bell sounded far off, they stopped work and sang the service where they were. If they were close home, they would hurry to the church, stopping a moment in the quiet cloister to put work out of their thoughts and remember only God. After Sext they worked until it was time to come back to the church for another service, *Nones*.

You must be wondering whether the monks ever had anything to eat. In winter they only had one meal a day and this came soon after Nones. You can imagine how hungry they must have been as they went through the cloister to the refectory (or frater), not forgetting to wash their hands as they went in. Inside, each monk bowed to the high-table and then stood in silence at his own proper place (the eldest next the high-table and the youngest by the door) until the Abbot or Prior came to his seat and rang the bell. When grace had been said, all sat down and the Reader began to read the Bible from the pulpit. Then the servers brought the dishes from the kitchen and began to serve, from the eldest down to the youngest. They were very careful about good manners at dinner. The monks serving had to be quick but not noisy; they must not bump each other's elbows or spill things. When eating, monks were told not to wipe their fingers or knives on the tablecloth nor put their fingers in their cups. Once, when a monk made rude sucking noises when eating his porridge, the others thought it was a little devil doing this.

For food, each monk was allowed one pound of bread and one mug of beer each day. Besides this there were two dishes of cooked vegetables or soup or porridge for dinner, but never any meat or fish or eggs. Sometimes they had green salad or cheese or fruit, but there was not much variety. Once, when a monk was asked what he had to eat, he said cheerfully: "Yesterday I had peas and *pot-herbs*, today pot-herbs and peas; tomorrow I shall eat peas with my pot-herbs, and the day after, pot-herbs with my peas." The reader, the cook and the servers, because they had to wait for their dinner till afterwards, were allowed an early lunch beforehand of bread and beer, called *mixt*, and the novices and younger monks with big appetites were also allowed to have mixt, because they got so hungry waiting for dinner.

At the end of dinner the bell rang again and they all walked in procession to the church, singing the 51st Psalm. (What is it?) There they gave thanks to God for food and went back to the cloister for reading, or perhaps to the warming-house, until it was time for the service of *Vespers* at dusk. Soon after this the whole family of monks and lay brothers gathered in the cloister to end the day together. While the last light faded, one of the monks read aloud from a good book, and then, with thoughts quietly turning to God again after the day's work, the Abbot gave the signal for them all to go into church for the last service, *Compline*.

In summer the programme was a little different. Then there was much work to be done outdoors, so they got up earlier and sang Vigils and Lauds close together. Prime followed quickly and then their chapter-meeting. After this they hurried out to work. When work was urgent at hay-time or harvest, they would say Tierce, Sext and even Nones in the fields. Because of the hard, outdoor work, they were allowed two meals a day, and because the night was shorter, they had a midday sleep. So dinner came after Sext, then an hour's sleep in the dorter, then work again. Some monks would take their dinner and their rest in the fields. Supper came after Vespers, and Compline not till eight o'clock, but before it was dark they would be going to their beds.

So the year went round—summer and winter—in an orderly way, and, except for special days of fasting or feasting, the monks always knew what they would be doing at each hour. Their days were spent in praising God

30

either in church or cloister or field, and most of them were well content.

Now let me explain about the lay brothers. They were not so learned as the monks, for they could not read or write, but they came to the monastery because they wanted to serve God with their hands. Like the monks, they took solemn vows, but they had much less to learn, for they did not sing such long services. In the morning they got up rather later than the monks, said their own services quietly in their own part of the church, up to Prime, and then went out to work in field or workshop. During the day they stood in the fields or wherever they happened to be at the time of Tierce, Sext and None, to say the special prayers and psalms they had learnt. At night they generally came back and joined with the monks for Compline, the last service. They had their meals in their own refectory and, because of their hard work, they were allowed half a pound of the best bread for mixt (which was early lunch, you remember) and as much coarse bread as they liked. They had their own chapter-meeting (but only three times a year) and their own dorter. They dressed a little differently from the monks, wearing a tunic, stockings, boots, hood and cloak. So if you had met one of them in the fields, you would have known by his clothes that he was a lay brother.

DAILY WORK AT RIEVAULX

THE Cistercians believed in hard work as well as prayer. St. Bernard was determined to go back to the very first days of the Benedictine monks when they had ploughed and reaped, cooked and served, and done all their own work. So he said that the Cistercian monasteries were to be away in the wilderness, where there were no labourers to help them and where the monks had to start right from the beginning in growing their food.

When Ailred first went to Rievaulx it was still wild and rough, but the monks were busy turning the wilderness into a garden. Day after day monks and lay brothers would gather at the abbey gate with their axes and spades, the Abbot would come to bless the tools, and they would go forth to some rough and stony place or thick forest, to break up the rocks, cut down trees and thorns, and dig the ground. In the valley, when the stones were cleared, they could plough and then sow corn. By the river in summer-time they could make good hay. Close to the monastery they could plant a garden for vegetables and fruit.

But they could not grow crops on the steep and stony hillsides. What do you think these could be used for? The Cistercian monks found the right answer: SHEEP. Wiry sheep that scrambled about on the hills produced very good wool, and the monks, of course, needed wool for their habits and other clothes. So they began to keep sheep. By and by they had large flocks grazing up the *dale*.

In summer each year these were all driven down for the sheep-washing and shearing. Soon the monks found they were getting more and more sacks of wool, far more than they needed for themselves. So they began to sell some, and soon Cistercian wool from Yorkshire was so famous that wool-merchants were coming from over the seas to buy it.

Bit by bit the monks tamed the wild dale, until you could look right up it and see nothing but rich green fields, tidy woods and smooth hillsides dotted with white sheep. Through the middle of the valley there flowed the River Ric, like a silver snake. Sometimes, when they looked out and remembered what it had been like when they arrived, the monks were reminded of a verse in the Bible: *The desert shall rejoice and blossom as the rose.* Can you find this verse in a Bible?

As time went on, people gave them more land, sometimes a long way from the monastery, so that, when they were working there, they could not get back to church for all the services. When the hours of the services came round, the monks would listen for the Abbey bell and then, standing among the haycocks or corn-sheaves, with their tools laid all round them, they would sing the psalms and prayers as if they were in church. There was one verse from Psalm 128 they liked to sing in the fields: *For thou shalt eat the labour of thine hands, happy shalt thou be, and it shall be well with thee.* Some of the lands they were given were so far away that they could not get back at night. So here they built small farms or *granges* where monks and lay brothers could live for a few days.

Of course the monks needed iron for tools and various other things. A man named Adam Fitzpiers gave them some iron mines and a place where they could smelt iron and forge all their tools. If the full monks had had all this work to do themselves, they would never have had the proper time for prayer and study. That is why the lay brothers were so important: by doing so much work, they set the monks free for part of the time to serve God in other ways.

Close to the abbey itself there were always many jobs to do. You can picture monks and lay brothers working in the blacksmith's forge, shoeing horses or mending plough-shares; feeding the oxen; thrashing corn in the great barn and grinding it in the mill; baking loaves in the bakehouse; making wooden benches in the carpenter's shed. Inside you might see them raking out the old straw in the dorter and putting down fresh, washing the stone pavement of the cloisters or their own clothes, carrying water or stacking sacks in the cellarium.

Then there were special duties for which the monks were chosen by the Abbot or Prior. The cooks were chosen every week and had the important task of seeing that all the food was well cooked and that everyone had enough. There were strict rules about the cooks' work. Each evening, when the bell rang for Vespers, the cooks went to the kitchen, measured out the beans for the bean-soup or *pottage* to be eaten next day, and washed them in three lots of water. They said their Vespers together in the kitchen and, before they went to bed, put the beans ready with water in the great boiling *cauldron*. After Lauds the next morning, the cooks washed themselves thoroughly and went to the kitchen to put the big pot on the fire. They had to watch it most carefully not to burn the beans. When the beans were all cooked, another big pot of water was put on the fire to heat, ready for the washing-up. Then the cooks would sit down in the kitchen and say

Tierce together. Next, they had to go to the daily chapter, but after this the beans were put on to boil again and another pot full of vegetables was also put on the fire. While the dinner was cooking only two cooks stayed to watch, but when the bell rang for dinner all the cooks as well as the servers were in the kitchen to serve out the pottage and other food. They put special sleeves on their arms not to spoil their habits. The cooks had strict orders to wash up all the plates in hot water as soon as they were finished with, so that greasy bits would not stick on.

We do not know just how many pots and pans they had at Rievaulx, but another monastery has left us a complete list:

3 cauldrons, one for beans, one for vegetables, one for washing-up water;
4 great dishes;
4 spoons, one for beans, one for vegetables, a small one for putting salt in the soup, a large iron one for shovelling coal on the fire;
4 pairs of sleeves for the servers;
2 pairs of gloves for holding hot dishes;
3 towels for wiping the plates (clean once a week);
several knives, and a stone for sharpening them;
2 ladles, a strainer, and a pair of *bellows*.

We must not forget that part of the monks' daily work was reading and writing books. In some monasteries they spent a lot of time copying beautiful books: if you look on page 68, you can find out more about them. But St. Bernard did not want his monks to spend too much time writing or copying books. He did want them, however, to read and think about the Bible, and sometimes they were allowed to write books—Ailred did, for one. So each day you would probably see some monks sitting in the

35

cloister with big books (much bigger than ours) on their wooden desks. Behind them the large, wooden book-cupboards, called *aumbries*, would be open and you would see heavy, leather-bound books on the shelves. Here is a monk sitting and thinking about what he has been reading:

To keep the monastery busy like a hive of bees, different officials were needed to manage different parts of it. These were chosen by the Abbot. First, there was the Prior, who helped the Abbot to rule the whole family of the monastery. He arranged the various tasks of the monks and saw that everything was done properly and at the right time. If anyone was getting slack about his duties the Prior would speak to him. At night he locked all the doors, took the keys with him up to the dorter and did not lie down until everyone else was in bed. In the morning he looked round sharply to see that no one overslept.

Above all, he had to keep the monks from quarrelling so that the house was at peace. The Abbot was the father of the monastery and the Prior the mother.

In charge of the church was the *Sacrist*. Since the church was the centre of the monastery, the Sacrist was an important man. He had to look after the holy bread and wine for the Mass, the robes or *vestments* which the Abbot and monks put on for Mass, and the hangings and cloth for the altar. All these he kept in cupboards in his little room, called

The Prior

the *sacristy*. In some monasteries they had splendid treasures of embroidered altar-fronts, silk hangings, robes of cloth of gold and velvet, golden, jewelled crucifixes, *chalices* and so on. St. Bernard thought that many monks cared more about their grand and beautiful churches than about worshipping God, so he said that everything in a Cistercian church was to be very plain. The hangings were of plain linen, and so were the vestments. Embroidery, gold and jewels were strictly forbidden. Even the altar candlesticks must be of plain iron instead of gold and silver. Perhaps, when the sacrist was putting away these simple things, he sighed sometimes for gorgeous treasures, but he remembered that God was best worshipped with true hearts, not rich jewels.

The Sacrist had to see that the church was kept clean,

and he looked after the candles and lights, not only in the church but in the whole monastery. He bought the wax and *tallow* and saw that the candles were properly made. Very early in the morning, before Vigils, he had to get up and light candles for the dorter and four *cressets* in the cloister (these were bowls of tallow with lighted wicks floating in them). In the church he had to see that the altar candle was lighted and that there was a lighted lantern ready for those who read the lessons. If it was very dark, he had to provide candles for the novices who did not yet know the psalms by heart. Most of the monks needed no lights, for they could chant the services with their eyes shut. Perhaps most important of all, the Sacrist had to sound the bell for all the services in church.

Nearly as important as the Sacrist was the *Precentor* or *Cantor*, who was in charge of the music. He trained the novices to sing and chant in the right way and he chose all the music for the services. In church he sat in a special seat and led the singing. Sometimes he would conduct it with his staff. Here he is taking a choir practice. When the monks went round the monastery singing in procession, the Precentor would walk up

and down the line to keep the singing together. He also used to hear beforehand the monks who had to read aloud in church or at dinner, to make sure that they could do it without stumbling. Beside all this, he looked after the books, arranging them on the shelves and seeing that they were put back in the right places. He had to watch to see that they did not get damp or eaten by mice; when they were torn he had to get them mended. He also used to mix the ink (for there were no ready-mixed bottles of ink to buy in those days) and get ready the *parchment* on which they wrote. This was not paper but the skin of sheep or calf, scraped and rubbed until all the hair was off and it was quite smooth and shiny. It was thicker than paper and rather scarce, so the monks nearly always wrote on both sides and often in small, close handwriting to save space.

Then, of course, there were all the officials who looked after practical things. First, the *Cellarer*. He was important because he had charge of all the stores for the monastery, especially the food and drink. A great deal of food was grown in their own fields, but the Cellarer had to see that there was enough corn, flour, beans and other things in the bins and, when they were getting empty, bring in more from the barns or from the more distant granges. At dinner he stood by the kitchen hatch to see that enough food was handed through and that it was good. Sometimes he had to travel away to market to buy salt and other things which the monks could not grow or make themselves. But he never went away without the permission of the Abbot, and when he was at market or visiting a grange, he always said the proper services at the right time by himself. Of course he had to keep the stores locked up, so

he always carried a large key. Here is a Cellarer with his key and money-bag.

The *Kitchener*, as you can guess, looked after the cooks. It was important to have good cooking, so the Abbot and Prior used to choose the Kitchener together and they tried to pick out a monk who would be neither mean nor extravagant with food. He had to see that there was enough and that it was all well cooked. He also had to see that all the plates and dishes were clean and not cracked. In the refectory a monk called the *Refectorian* looked after everything. He had to see that the floor was covered with rushes, that there were flowers or sweet-smelling plants on the tables, and that by each monk's place there was his loaf of bread, wrapped in a clean napkin, his cup and his spoon. He had also to see that the salt was dry, and that there was hot water and clean towels ready for the monks to wash their hands before dinner. Every day he had to count the spoons and cups and see that they were clean.

The *Infirmarian* was in charge of the sick and old monks who live in the Infirmary. I think you would know without my telling you that the *Guest-master* looked after the guest-house and entertained visitors, while the Novice-master taught the novices. At the gate was the Porter: he had to be a wise monk who knew how to answer visitors politely and whether he ought to let people in or out.

The monks themselves were forbidden to wander outside unless the Abbot or Prior sent them on an errand. When strangers knocked, the Porter decided if they were the sort to let in. Here are some Cistercian monks welcoming a visitor. As a sign that he is important, they hide their hands in their sleeves.

Finally, there was the *Almoner*, who gave food and clothes to poor people. The monks believed that people in need belonged especially to Christ—Christ's poor they called them. So the Almoner was told to be ready to help any poor people who came knocking at the gate, though he must try not to be taken in by frauds. Every day the servers in the refectory collected in a basket all the pieces of bread left over and gave this to the Almoner for hungry folk. He also got all the monks' old habits for those who came shivering with cold in winter-time.

Now I have told you about all the chief officials in the monastery. When a monk was chosen for one of these jobs he was specially blessed for this work, and when he made a mistake or did something badly, he asked the pardon of all his brothers. These duties were thought of as part of the service of God and all work done in the monastery was done to the glory of God.

HOW AILRED BECAME ABBOT OF RIEVAULX

AILRED lived the life of a monk with great gladness. When he prayed or sang psalms, he did it with all his might, and when he worked in the kitchen, he also did it with all his might. He had a great friend, named Walter Daniel, who wrote all he knew of Ailred after he was dead. This is what he says about the way Ailred worked:

> Not with noisy show before the others, with unseemly fuss, jostling the monks on all sides and banging the shoulders of the brethren, but turning gaily to whatever he was told to do. He began and ended the task just as he was bidden, neither more nor less. He never asked the Prior to excuse him a task or let him do something else. He did not spare the soft skin of his hands but manfully wielded with his slender fingers the rough tools of the field work.

So Ailred ploughed and reaped and washed up in the kitchen until his hands were rough and red. Another of his friends was a young monk named Simon. They could not talk to each other because of the rule of silence, but Ailred once said: "His face, his way of walking, his very silence spoke to me." I wonder if you would find it very difficult not to talk to your best friend? Simon died while still young, but Ailred always remembered him.

Abbot William soon discovered that Ailred was a wise young man, so he often called him to his seat in the cloister to ask his help about difficult problems. Once he sent him on a long journey to the Pope in Rome. When he came back, the Abbot made him Novice-master. The novices never had a better master. He taught them all they had to know: first, how to put on their habits and how to behave properly in the dorter and the refectory, to bow to the Abbot and Prior, to be respectful to older monks and not to laugh too much; then the Rule and the prayers and psalms they had to learn by heart; then how to read the Bible in Latin and how to chant and sing correctly; above all, how to keep silence and obey.

Often the boys or young men who were novices were worried and anxious. Perhaps they had very much wanted to be monks but when they began their training they found life very hard. Ailred was the kind of master to whom they could easily tell their troubles. This is what one novice said to him: "Before I came here I could never have kept silent for so long and given up all the gossiping I loved so much. I used to do whatever I liked, laugh and chatter with my friends, go to rich feasts, drink much wine and sleep late in the mornings."

Then Ailred said: "And what do you do now?" And the novice smiled and said: "Oh now, how different it is! Now my food is very little, my clothes are rough and my drink is water from the spring. I sleep, tired out with work, on a hard mat, and just when sleep is sweetest, the sound of the bell makes me get up. I can only talk to three men, and even then as little as possible, and I obey my masters just like an animal, going where I am told and doing what I am told. And yet—here there are no grumblings and quarrellings, here everything is shared equally

43

and three hundred men cheerfully obey one master (the Abbot)."

"You must not think that everyone in the monastery is perfect," said Ailred, "But tell me, would you like to go back to the old life now?" And the reply was, "Never!"

Ailred trained himself as well as the novices. He thought it was good training to be hard on his body. So he found a place where a cold spring of water bubbled up and there he made a kind of bath where he used to sit in the icy water until his body was quite numb. But he never told anyone and the rest of the monks only found out later what he was doing.

By and by Ailred was chosen to be the Abbot of a new monastery just started at Revesby in Lincolnshire. So for

a few years he went away from Rievaulx. The time came when old Abbot William died and the monks of Rievaulx met solemnly in chapter to elect a new abbot. They chose a monk named Maurice, but after two years he said he would rather go back to being a simple monk. Then they chose Ailred as the third abbot. So Ailred became Abbot or Father of the family at Rievaulx. We have no picture of Ailred, but here is one of another Abbot, wearing a *mitre* on his head and carrying a staff, as Ailred would have done.

44

All the monks had to honour and obey him. In the chapter-house or refectory they would stand up until he came in. When he passed in the cloister, they would stand up and bow. At dinner he was the only monk who could ask for something special to eat. But Ailred would never ask for himself; sometimes, if he thought one of the monks needed a little extra, he would send for it and the monk would rise and bow his thanks. Although everyone was so respectful, Ailred always remembered that the honour was not given to him but to Christ, the unseen head of the monastery.

Ailred wanted to make it easy for people to come and join the monastery. So the gates were wide open and men of all kinds came flocking in. One was the old knight Walter Espec, who, when his fighting days were over, came to be a monk at Rievaulx which he had helped to build. Some who came were ill, some unhappy, some were strangers from foreign lands. Ailred refused no one. "All, weak or strong," he used to say, "shall find here (like the fishes in the wide sea) peace and plenty of room." So many came that before Ailred died there were 140 monks and 500 lay brothers. On special feast-days, when everyone came to church, there were so many that they were packed together like bees in a hive (or, as we should say, like sardines). Sundays and feast-days were joyful days at Rievaulx. On Sundays they went in procession from the church all round the monastery—through the cloister, dorter, refectory, cellarium, etc.—singing psalms as they went. On page 3 you will see one of the processions going round the monastery.

Ailred had many things to look after. When he became Abbot, the monastery was still only half-built, and before long so many new monks were coming in that they had to enlarge what had been already built. They found another quarry of good stone where they could slide the stones downhill and then float them down the river. To do this properly they dammed up the river and made the canal longer. With this stone, and with oak logs which they cut and floated down too, the monks enlarged the chapter-house and cloister and did a lot of other building. Ailred must often have been busy making plans or inspecting the monks who were builders or seeing the stone floated down on rafts.

Once each year he had to travel across the sea to Citeaux to a general meeting with St. Bernard of all the Cistercian Abbots. Ailred also used to visit all the monasteries that Rievaulx had started, her daughter houses, as they were called. Of course, you must not think of modern travel by motor or train or aeroplane. Ailred would take many weeks travelling slowly on horseback along rough tracks. Men were glad to see him everywhere he went. Perhaps he looked rather like this Abbot who has put a hat over his hood to shade him from the hot sun:

What Ailred enjoyed most was staying at home in the lovely and peaceful Rievaulx, writing books and helping the monks to live holy lives. St. Bernard asked him to write about his life as a monk, and he called this book THE MIRROR OF LOVE. After this he wrote many other books. Sometimes he wrote about his friends and we can almost hear him talking to them sweetly and quietly. The monks must have loved to visit him. Some Abbots were always bustling about on business, far too busy to stop. Not so Ailred: if any monk was worried or puzzled, he could tell his troubles to the Abbot. If a monk just wanted to listen while Ailred talked of the wonder of God's love, the Abbot always seemed to have time. One day his friend, Walter Daniel, got very cross while Ailred was doing business with some men. He sat in the corner, tugging his hair and looking daggers, until Ailred said: "Come now, we must put up with interruptions! See, they have gone now and we can talk of higher things." Even when he was ill, Ailred never told the monks to go away, but let them sit by, or even on, his bed while he taught them.

For the last four years of his life Ailred was ill and lived in a special little house built for him. He suffered much pain but was always patient and cheerful. When the time came for him to die, all the monks stood close round their beloved father. He was happy, for he died at home. "Let me die in my little nest," a monk once wrote, and so Ailred did.

While he was Abbot, Ailred wrote a prayer asking God to make him a good Abbot or shepherd, guarding his monks like a flock of sheep. On the next page is part of his prayer:

O Good Shepherd Jesus!
good, gentle, tender Shepherd!
Behold a shepherd, poor and pitiful,
a shepherd of Thy sheep indeed,
but weak and clumsy and of little use,
        cries out to Thee.
To Thee, I say, Good Shepherd,
this shepherd who is not good, makes his prayer.

   . . . .

Thou hast given Thy sinful servant
the task of ruling them.

My God, Thou knowest what a fool I am.

Therefore, sweet Lord, I ask Thee, not for gold,
I ask Thee not for silver, nor for jewels,
but only that Thou wouldst give me wisdom,
that I may know how to rule Thy people well.

Send Wisdom from Thy throne of might
to be with me, to work with me,
to act with me, to speak with me.

Rievaulx from the air, showing some parts built after Ailred's time.

THE STORY OF FOUNTAINS ABBEY

Do YOU remember that the first band of White Monks from France rested in the great Benedictine monastery of St. Mary's at York before they went on to Rievaulx? Now the monks of St. Mary's had been getting very slack in keeping the Rule. They were living too comfortably, and this worried some of them. "How can we serve God properly when we do not keep St. Benedict's Rule?" they said. When they saw how strict these new Cistercian visitors were, they were still more ashamed and persuaded their leader, Prior Richard, to speak to the Abbot. Richard said to him: "We break the Rule all the time. We wander about chattering to each other when we ought to be keeping silence. We eat all kinds of delicacies and drink delightful drinks which we are really forbidden to touch. We lose our tempers, we quarrel, we please ourselves, we make merry, we grow fat. Let us then copy the example of these new men of God who have come from Cîteaux, and go back to our proper Rule!"

Now Abbot Godfrey was an old man who enjoyed his comfortable life and did not want to change. He was scared of the idea of starting to live like the Cistercian monks, so he threatened to punish Prior Richard and his friends if they said any more. This only made them keener in their desire. They went to the Archbishop of York, named Thurstan. When he had heard their story, he came with a great crowd of priests to see old Abbot Godfrey. Even men of God lose their tempers sometimes and there was a disgraceful fight at the chapter-house door when Abbot

Godfrey, with most of the monks, tried to push out the Archbishop and his followers, as they tried to push in. Finally the Archbishop went away, taking with him thirteen monks who wanted to keep the strict Rule, and leaving old Abbot Godfrey to settle down with the rest to their comfortable ways again. I expect they sighed with relief and said: "Thank goodness those disturbers of the peace have gone!" Here is Archbishop Thurstan looking rather stern.

Now the thirteen monks were homeless. They had nothing except the habits they wore. At first the Archbishop gave them a home in York. Then he gave them a piece of land in a wild and lonely place on which to build their monastery. There were only twelve by this time, for one had been tempted back from the hard life to the easy-going ways at St. Mary's. The twelve elected Prior Richard as their Abbot and set out after Christmas, in the dead of winter, to find their piece of land.

It was a hard time to start, a time of ice and snow and bitter winds. When they found their place in Skeldale it was covered with thorn bushes and surrounded by jagged rocks, a place for wild beasts rather than men. But in the middle there was a great elm-tree and under it they tried to find shelter. At first they could only huddle together under some straw to keep warm, but bit by bit they built little wooden huts thatched with heather. They kept the Rule steadfastly: at the proper times they stood under their elm-tree to sing the services, just as if they were in a solemn church. They ate bread which the Archbishop Thurstan sent them and drank water from the river. All the time they worked hard—cutting wood, building huts, plaiting mats with rushes, clearing away thorns and rocks, digging the ground and sowing crops. No one rested until he was weary with work. Hungry they went to meals and weary to bed, yet never grumbling. No sign of sadness was seen, but they blessed God cheerfully, poor in worldly goods but rich in faith.

But after a while Archbishop Thurstan could send them no more bread. Their own crops had not yet grown, so they had often to pick leaves from the trees and plants and stew these with salt for their dinner. One day a poor traveller knocked at the gate, begging in the name of Christ for a piece of bread. The porter said that they had none, but the poor man begged so piteously that the porter went to the Abbot, who called the brother in charge of the bread. He shook his head, saying that he had only two and a half loaves which he was saving for the carpenter-monks who were building a wooden chapel. "Then," said the Abbot, "do thou give one loaf to the poor man and keep what is left for the carpenters. For the rest of us, the Lord will provide something." So the beggar took the loaf, and lo! just as he was going, there came up to the gate two men dragging a cart full of fine white loaves, a present from a knight who had heard that the monks were starving! "Truly, God is good," said the monks, "for in return for one loaf of coarse flour, He has sent us many loaves of fine white flour!"

So the monks in Skeldale struggled on. They were so poor that at one moment they nearly gave up, but just then a rich man named Hugh decided to join them and he brought with him waggons full of chairs, tables, beds and books, as well as all his money. When they saw all these riches they rejoiced; part they gave to the poor and with the rest they furnished their huts and bought stone to build a proper church and cloister. By this time they had decided to join St. Bernard's family of Cistercian monasteries.

Down by the river, in the midst of the valley, they began to build their monastery. Because the only music they heard in that quiet place was the tinkle of little streams running down the hillsides to join the river, they called it Fountains Abbey. Soon many people began to hear of the cheerful poverty and strict lives of these monks. Men came to join them and brought their wealth; others gave them land, until they were able to build a beautiful church

Fountains Abbey today.

and monastery and turn the whole wild valley into pleasant green fields.

One of the men who brought his gold and silver to Fountains Abbey and became a monk there was named Serlo. When he was an old man he wrote down all he could remember and all he had been told about those early days, when the first twelve lived under the elm-tree, while they were building their great abbey. And so it is that we know the story of Fountains Abbey because Serlo wrote it down.

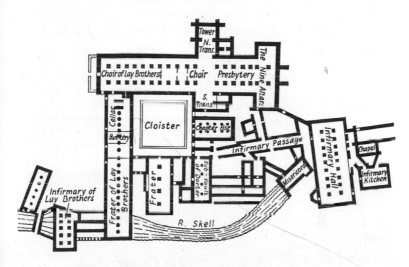

Plan of Fountains Abbey.

Can you find the 'sub-vault of dorter'? The dorter was built over this, extending right over the chapter-house to the church.

HERE YOU CAN FIND OUT MORE ABOUT MONKS AND MONASTERIES IN ENGLAND

THE DIFFERENT KINDS OF MONKS

The Benedictine or *Black Monks*

These were the first families of monks who followed St. Benedict's Rule and did not make any great changes in it. They wore a white woollen gown and over this a black habit and *cowl* (hood). There is a picture of a Black Monk on p. 7 and here is another.

The Cluniac Monks

These belonged to a family of monks which started at Cluny in France and founded daughter houses all over Europe. They followed St. Benedict's Rule but made changes in it. They wore a habit very like the Benedictine one and looked like this.

The Cistercian or White Monks

These, as you know, belonged to a family of monks which had its centre at Citeaux, and tried to keep the Rule of St. Benedict very strictly. Their great teacher was St. Bernard and they founded many houses all over Europe. You can remind yourself of what they looked like by turning to p. 9.

The Carthusian Monks

They belonged to a family of monks which started at the Grande Chartreuse in France. On p. 75 you can read the story of how they began. They lived by a stricter rule than the Benedictines or even the Cistercians, and each monk spent much time alone in silent study and prayer. They wore a white gown and cowl, and over the gown a white *scapular* (piece of cloth hanging down at back and front). Here is a Carthusian monk.

These were the most important families of monks, though, of course, there were others.

Canons and Friars

Then there were families of canons who lived a life rather like the monks' but under a different rule. The most important family of canons was named after St. Augustine, *Augustinian (or Austin) canons.*

There was one specially English family of the *Gilbertines* called after their founder St. Gilbert of Sempringham. There was also a family with the long name of *Praemonstratensian canons*.

Later than the monks and canons came the friars. They did not live all the time in one place, as did the monks, and they often went around preaching to the ordinary people in the market-places or churchyards.

They had their own rules, but these were different from the Rule of St. Benedict. The most important families of friars were:

The Franciscans or *Friars Minor*, founded by St. Francis. They wore grey-brown tunics with a knotted cord round the waist and a black cowl. They were often called Grey Friars.

The Dominicans or *Friars Preacher*, founded by St. Dominic. They wore a white tunic and scapular, and on top a black cloak and cowl. They were often called Black Friars.

There was also a family of Augustinian (or Austin) friars.

Grey Friar.

Black Friar.

56

Here is a plan of Beaulieu Abbey in the South of England. If
you look at it carefully, you will see that it is arranged on the same
kind of plan as Rievaulx and Fountains in the North of England.
There were often some little differences, but generally monasteries
were arranged on much the same plan.

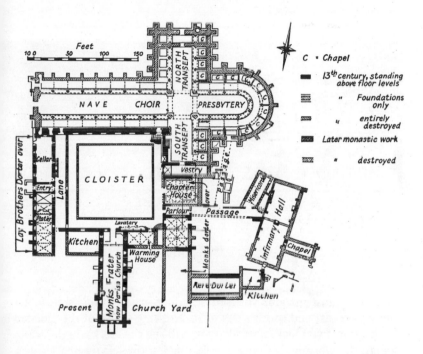

In many different parts of England you can visit famous monasteries, though most of them—alas—are now in ruins. If you live
near one, go and visit it, and as you stand in the empty place, try
to think of it full of monks living the kind of life that Ailred lived
at Rievaulx.

The next pictures show you parts of different monasteries, as they look today. Think of what the monks would have been doing in that particular place, as you look at each one.

Part of Cleeve Abbey.

Here you must imagine yourself standing inside the cloister, looking at the east and south sides of it. Nothing is left of the cloister walks, but if you look carefully, you will see the marks on the walls where the cloister roof once joined on. On the left (the east side), the big archway leads into the chapter-house, and the staircase next to it goes up to the dorter, to which all the narrow windows you can see belong. How many are there? On the south side (the right), the beautiful windows belong to the frater. Can you see the staircase up to it? By the staircase-foot is a trough for washing hands and one of the small doors leads into the warming-house.

Cloister at Gloucester.

Here you will see that along the side nearest the light, the cloister has been divided by wooden partitions into separate little rooms, called *carrels*, where the monks could read and write books sheltered from the sharp winds that blew along the cloister.

And here is a picture of another cloister, in a plainer and earlier style, built at Fontenay in France:

Chapter House at Buildwas.

You must imagine here a stone seat all round the walls for the monks to sit on during their morning chapter, and a special, higher seat for the Abbot.

Frater at Cleeve.

Tintern Abbey.

This is one of the most famous abbeys in England. In this picture
you are looking down the nave of the church to the west end. Many
people have stood here and thought how beautiful it was with the
blue sky roofing it and ivy spreading up the pillars. But still more,
they have thought, how wonderful it must have been when the
monks sang God's praises here in a church which was not a ruin!

Some of the Things St. Benedict said to his Monks in his Rule

1. We are now going to start a school for the service of God in which we hope nothing harsh or burdensome will be demanded. In living our life by the growth of faith, the path of God's commandments is run with unspeakable loving sweetness, so that, never leaving His school, but persevering in the monastery until death, we share by our patience in the sufferings of Christ and so are made fit to share in His glory.

2. Whenever anything important has to be decided in the monastery, let the Abbot call together all the family. After hearing the advice of the brothers, let him make up his own mind. And let the brothers give their opinions humbly and presume not stiffly to argue for their own views. Prompt obedience is required of all monks. They live not as they themselves would choose, but, following the command of another speedily, they agree to be ruled by the Abbot.

3. Eight times a day let us give praise to our Creator, that is, at Vigils, Lauds, Prime, Tierce, Sext, None, Vespers, and Compline.

4. All the monks shall sleep in separate beds. If it is possible, let them all sleep in a common dorter. Let a candle be always burning in the room until morning and let the monks sleep in their clothes and girdles, but they are not to have knives by their sides in bed lest they injure themselves by accident while sleeping. They shall always be ready to rise quickly when the signal is given and hasten to the Divine Office. The younger brothers are not to have their beds next to each other but among those of the elders. And let them rouse the sleepy-heads and help them to get up.

5. No one shall keep as his own anything whatever: neither book nor writing-tablet nor pen: nothing at all.

6. The brothers are so to serve each other that no one be excused from the work of the kitchen. On Saturday he who ends his weekly service must clean up everything. He must wash the towels with which the brothers wipe their hands and feet, and he who finishes his service and he who begins are to wash the feet of all the rest. Let him who is finishing his week say: "Blessed art Thou, O Lord God, who didst help me," and let him who is beginning his week say: "O Lord, make haste to help me."

7. Monks shall practise silence at all times, but especially at night-time. So, on coming out from Compline, no one shall be allowed to speak at all.

8. Let the brothers be given clothes suitable to the climate, for in cold places more is needed and less in warm. In ordinary places it will be enough for each monk to have a cowl and habit, in winter the cowl being of thicker stuff. He should also have a scapular to work in and shoes and stockings for the feet. Monks must not grumble about the colour or rough material of their clothes. When getting new ones, they must always give back the old to be kept for the poor. It is enough for a monk to have two habits and two cowls; anything more is extravagant. A mattress, blanket, coverlet and pillow are enough for bedding.

9. Do thou, therefore, whoever thou art who hasteneth forward to the heavenly country, accomplish first, by the help of Christ, this little Rule written for beginners, and then at length shalt thou come, under God's guidance, to the lofty heights of belief and virtue.

Archbishop Lanfranc's Rules for Monks

In the days of King William the Conqueror a great Archbishop of Canterbury named Lanfranc made a book of rules for his monks at Canterbury which was also used by many other monasteries. In this book he made a careful time-table for the monks which was different in winter and summer. Here is part of his time-table:

On the first of October the monks shall stop the midday sleep which they take in summer-time. They shall rise in night habit and shoes to sing Matins and then sit and pray in the choir until Lauds is sung. Then they shall return to bed. When day is breaking, the small bell shall be rung softly. Then the brothers, rising in their night shoes, and the children with lanterns shall enter the church to sing Prime. After this they shall sit in the cloister and the children shall begin by reading aloud and afterwards, if need be, practise the chant. Before Tierce no one shall put on his day shoes, except those who have work to do outside the cloister. When it is nearly time for Tierce, the sacristan shall sound softly the smallest bell (called the *squilla*) and all shall go to the dorter, put on their day shoes and take their knives. The monks shall go to the church and wait on their knees while the children are washing. When they have washed and begun to comb their hair, the large bell shall ring for Tierce. Then the children shall enter the church and Tierce shall be sung.

When it is time for chapter, the Prior shall sound the squilla and at once all shall go to the chapter-house, walking in order of age two by two. After chapter the board shall be rapped and when the Abbot has said "Bless ye the Lord," talking is allowed in the cloister. The children shall hold a chapter of their own and afterwards go to the refectory to eat the children's breakfast (called mixt). Then Sext is sung and there is talking in the cloister again until High Mass.

The rest of Lanfranc's October time-table was rather like the one at Rievaulx. On November first the winter time-table started. The most important change was that the monks did not go back to bed again between Lauds and Prime but stayed in the church to pray. You can guess how difficult it was to keep awake and so Lanfranc made this next rule.

During the time between Lauds and Prime the Prior shall go round the choir and other parts of the church with a lantern to see that no one has fallen asleep. If he finds someone praying, he shall pass by in silence, but if he finds a sleeper, he shall wake him. The children shall be carefully looked after by their masters in the chapter-house with lights burning, practising the chants.

(You see, they had no chance of sleeping!)

In Lanfranc's summer time-table the monks went to bed later and got up very early for Lauds, so he allowed them to go back to bed between Lauds and Prime and he also gave them a midday sleep.

In summer-time after dinner, they shall rest on their beds for the noonday sleep. When the ninth hour is near, the sacristan shall ring the small bell gently and all shall rise and wash their faces and hands and comb their hair. Then they shall go to the church and sit in choir. When the children have washed and begun to go to the towels, the sacristan shall ring the big bell, and when the children have entered the choir, they shall sing None.

(I hope the cold water woke them all up properly.)

64

Remember that Lanfranc wrote his rules for Black monks, so they were not quite the same as those for the White monks at Rievaulx. Did you notice two differences: (1) the Black monks were allowed to talk in the cloister sometimes; (2) there were children in the monastery? You can read more about the children below.

Some rules for monks about good manners at mealtimes

No noise must be made; if there are nuts, they are not to be cracked with the teeth, but opened quietly with the knife. If a monk spills anything, he must go and do penance in the middle of the refectory. He must not make signs across the room or lean on the table. His tongue and his eyes are to be kept in check. The servers must serve the food quickly but not running or jumping in an unbecoming fashion. The dishes must not be broken or dirty or smeared underneath. The server should use both hands and carry only one dish at a time. The monks must be careful not to wipe their noses or rub their teeth on the napkins or tablecloths.

And especially for young monks:

The youthful monk is bidden to wash his hands before meals, to keep his knife sharp and to say his grace. He must not seize on the vegetables or dip his own spoon in the common dish or put gravy in his mouth with his knife.

Rules for Boy Monks

Sometimes parents would offer their children to be dedicated to the service of God. They would bring them to the monastery and leave them there to grow up as monks. Here are some of the rules made for boys in a Benedictine monastery (Cistercian houses would not take children):

When a boy is offered for the holy order, let his parents bring him to the altar and wrap the boy's right hand in the altar-cloth. Then, having kissed it, let them put it into the hands of the monk who is receiving the boy and make the sign of the Cross over his head. Then let the Abbot pour holy water on his head and cut his hair with the shears round his neck, while the Precentor sings the psalm *Preserve me, O God*. Then let the boy take off his own clothes and be clothed in the habit and cowl, while the Abbot says: "May the Lord clothe thee!"

In the dorter let the masters sleep between every two boys, and sit between every two boys at other times. When they lie down in bed, let a master always be among them with his rod or at night with a candle. In the early morning, before the other monks wake, the Master of the Boys should rise very softly and just touch each of the children gently with his rod that they may wake from sleep. Then let them rise quickly. If any chance to loiter after the rest, he is at once to be smartly touched with the rod. This is their only punishment, either to be whipped with the rod or to have their hair stoutly pulled; never should they be kicked or hit.

When they sit in cloister or chapter, let each one have his own tree-trunk for a seat and so far apart that they cannot touch each other. If one of them sings badly at Vespers because he is sleepy, let the master give him a large, heavy book to hold to wake him up.

Indeed, any king's son could not be brought up more carefully in his palace than a boy in a well-ordered monastery.

A monastery school.

Monks who did not keep the rules

It was very easy to get slack and not keep the Rule strictly. Monks knew this, and so in one abbey church they carved a list of ten chief sins of monks, just to remind themselves:

1. Thinking too much about comfort.
2. Being tempted by rich food.
3. Making a noise in the cloister.
4. Quarrelling in chapter.
5. Being disorderly in church.
6. Being careless.
7. Being disobedient when novices.
8. Being lazy when old.
9. Wanting your own way.
10. Thinking worldly thoughts.

St. Bernard writes about monks who lived too comfortably

In those first days when the monastic life began, who would have believed that monks could live like this? Dish after dish is put on the table and, if they are not allowed meat, they get twice as much in mighty fishes. Who may tell of the eggs alone, in how many ways they are cooked, tossed, beaten to froth, now hard-boiled, now fried, now baked, now stuffed? Even though you eat quite enough in the first course, when the second comes you have to eat as much again because it is so tasty, and so with the third and fourth and even fifth!

Making excuses for themselves

When they made mistakes or broke the Rule, monks often thought that little invisible devils were doing the mischief. This is what some monks wrote about these devils:

All our little daily slips and mistakes are their doing. Sometimes they make my hands so heavy that I can hardly raise them. When we snore or cough or sneeze in church, it is their work. One troop of devils will spend all their efforts weighting my eyes and closing my eyelids, and another will come and snore in front of my nose, so that the brother next to me thinks I am doing it. The other day I saw a devil carefully plastering up a brother's ears so that he should not listen to the Rule being read in chapter.

In church the devils make us sing badly. One day, when the Abbot's choir was beginning the first psalm for Matins, the devils came crowding in and, by going to and fro, made the brothers quickly break down in the singing. When the other side of the choir tried to put them right, the devils, flying across, so disturbed them that they no longer knew what they were singing, and soon each side was shouting against the other. At last the psalm was somehow ended after much difficulty and confusion; then the devils departed and peace once more descended on the singers.

One night, when the Precentor began the psalm and the monk next to him took it up on rather a low note, the others joined in on the same note. But a not-very-wise young monk in the lower part of the choir, being annoyed that the psalm was begun too slow, started singing it five notes higher. Some helped him, some tried to stick to the lower note, some stopped singing altogether because of the dreadful noise, but he went on shouting the higher note at the top of his voice. Then the Prior saw a devil like a white-hot iron come out of the mouth of the monk who had started the higher note and fly across to the other side. And he knew the cause of all the mischief!

HOW MONKS MADE BEAUTIFUL BOOKS

Every monastery needed books, but there were no bookshops from which to buy them and—worse still—no printing presses  to print them. So they were written by hand by the monks themselves, and that is why we call the monks' books *manuscripts—manu* means in Latin *by hand, script* means *written*. A monk who was good at writing might sit for many days at a desk in the cloister carefully copying out page after page. In some monasteries there was a special room, called a *scriptorium*, where the writers could work more comfortably. Here is a picture of a monk at his desk.

To make a book the monks had to start at the very beginning by making their own ink and pens and smoothing the parchment or skin on which they wrote. The boys and young monks were taught to copy a certain handwriting so exactly that each letter was perfectly shaped. No scribbling was allowed! When their beautiful handwriting was perfect they might become *scribes* or copiers. The most important books to be copied were those used in the church services—Bibles, books of Psalms (called *Psalters*), and other books from which they sang the services. These all had to be written large so as to be easily read. The scribe would polish his piece of parchment and cut it the right size, then probably rule wide margins round all four sides and lines across on which to write. Slowly and carefully, with a steady hand, he would copy each line exactly, trying hard to make not one single mistake, for this was a book written for the glory of God. Here is a piece of beautiful handwriting by a monk:

Siquis autem urm indiget sapien
tia postulat a deo qui dat omnib;
affluenter & non improperat · & da
bitur ei · Postulet auté infide · m

Often the scribe would leave blanks for the capital letters and when he had finished the page he would give it to another monk who was clever at painting and was called an *illuminator*. This monk treasured very carefully a row of little paint pots full of rich, bright colours. He did not buy these in a shop but mixed them up for himself, using strange ingredients which were sometimes very rare and difficult to get.

This list tells you where some colours came from: crimson: the gum of a tree; scarlet: a tiny red insect; dragonsblood red: an Indian shrub; indigo blue: an Indian plant; woad blue: a plant grown in England; purple: a little shell-fish from the Mediterranean; green: copper mixed with the juice of rotten apples; yellow: saffron (crocus); gold: real gold.

69

The illuminator loved to draw elaborate capital letters and paint them in bright colours. Sometimes he put little pictures inside the capitals. Here is a beautiful capital showing a hero in the Bible who fought a bear and a lion. Find out his name.

Round the wide borders of the page the illuminator often painted a pattern like this.

So each page in the Bible or Psalter was made beautiful by long, careful hours of work, and slowly, page by page, the whole was finished, perhaps by several scribes and illuminators working for years. Finally, the monks would bind the pages together in a book with a rich cover, perhaps of velvet, ornamented with gold or silver or precious stones.

Here are some artists at work:

The books for the church were generally the largest and most beautiful, but monasteries needed many more books for the monks to study. So the scribes were always busy. These other books were not always written so carefully, and often the letters were smaller and the lines pushed close up together, for parchment was very expensive and they could not afford to waste it. Sometimes these books, too, would be illuminated with pictures and patterns. When they had been bound, often in brown leather, they would be ready to go into the book cupboard in the cloister, or into the special library which some monasteries built.

Sometimes monks became more than copiers of books, they were allowed to write their own books. The Abbot might say: "Will you start writing a history of our house, or the life of a holy man, or a book about the Bible?" The monk who was thus chosen would probably feel pleased and honoured, and he would settle down to long years of writing with joy, because he was allowed to serve God with his pen. So today we have many books written by monks, especially their histories, or *chronicles* as they were often called. There was one famous writer of chronicles at the abbey of St. Albans named Matthew Paris. He wrote books and books of history, and in one place (getting rather tired of always writing about other people) he drew a little picture of himself in the margin underneath a beautiful illuminated panel. Here it is:

Just now and then monks even wrote songs and made tunes for them. Some of our oldest Christmas carols were probably written by monks. In a book once belonging to Reading Abbey we have discovered a page on which a monk wrote an English song between some lines of Latin.

Can you recognize it? It is the famous song *Summer is i-cumen in.*

We do not know if the monk heard one of the country folk singing it or if he made it up for himself. Perhaps he looked out at the green meadows one fine spring day and felt it was so lovely that he must make a song. Anyway, he put it into his book and so he has left it for us to sing. Do you notice that the music notes are written in a funny way? Clever musicians today have discovered what these notes mean and so we are able to sing the monk's song about the gay cuckoo and the frolicking animals of springtime. I wonder if you sing this song in your school?

ENTERTAINING VISITORS

The Cistercians liked to put their monasteries in lonely places so that they should not be often disturbed by visitors, but many Benedictine houses were planned in towns or near big main roads. They got a great many visitors, for there were no hotels such as we have today, and so, at night-time, travellers looked for the nearest monastery at which they could sleep. Many of the monks liked having visitors—as long as there were not too many and they did not eat too extravagantly! They liked hearing travellers' tales and gossip, and if there was a monk writing a history he was eager to collect news to put in his book. On p. 76 you will read about a monk-historian named Orderic who enjoyed talking to knights about their fights; whenever visitors arrived, he came running with his writing table to scribble down whatever they could tell him. The great abbey of St. Albans was one of those on a main road—the great north road—and here travellers often stopped. So Matthew Paris (whom you read about on p. 72) was able to collect all kinds of news and fill volumes with his history.

Sometimes very important visitors—kings and queens, princes, bishops or barons—came to stay. These were generally entertained by the Abbot in his private lodging. He probably spent a terrible amount of money on food and wine to feast them, but hoped they would make the abbey a rich present when they left. More ordinary visitors were entertained in the guest-house, which was often a separate building outside the cloister on the west side, close to the big, main gate. This meant that travellers need not disturb the monks at work in the cloister. The Guest-master looked after these travellers. He had to keep the guest-house clean from spiders' webs and dirt and strew clean straw on the floors. Here is a list of all the things the Guest-master at Barnwell, near Cambridge, had to have ready for travellers:

      clean towels
      clean and untorn sheets
      mattresses, blankets and pillows
      quilts of a good size and pretty to look at
      cups which were not chipped
      silver spoons
      a basin which was clean inside and out
      candles and a candlestick
      a fire which did not smoke (in winter)
      clean salt in clean salt-cellars
      food served in clean bowls
      keys and locks to the doors and good bolts on the inside.

SOME STORIES OF MONKS GOOD AND BAD

How the Carthusian monks began

One night the Bishop of Grenoble (in France) saw in a dream seven suns coming together from different directions to the mountain called the Chartreuse. In the morning, while he was wondering what this dream meant, seven stately men, led by one called Bruno, arrived to ask if they could live up on the Chartreuse. Now this mountain is very high, and near the top is a deep, wild valley with many springs of water. Here they built seven separate cells in which to live. Every Sunday Bruno, the Prior, gave each man bread and *pulse* to last for the week, but for three days each week they lived on bread and water alone. No one, except the Prior, ever put a foot outside his cell, except to go to the church. All the time they spent reading and praying.

Told by Walter Map.

The Knight who became a Monk

There was once a knight named Walewan who wanted to be a monk. So he rode to the monastery on his war-horse in full armour. Still in full armour, he rode right into the cloister, dismounted, and marched right down the middle of the church with all his armour clanking as he went. Then, kneeling at the altar, he stripped it all off and asked to be clothed in the habit of a monk, for he thought it fit to lay down his earthly knighthood at the place where he wished to become a Knight of the Holy Spirit.

Told by Caesar of Heisterbach.

How a little boy was sent overseas to be a monk

There was once a little boy named Orderic. He lived by the river Severn at Shrewsbury, and his father, Ordelerius, was a Norman who had come over the sea from Normandy with Earl Roger Montgomery, one of William the Conqueror's barons. Perhaps Ordelerius married an English girl, for the little Orderic felt he belonged to England and lived happily with his father and mother until he was ten. But one day a strange monk named Rainald arrived from France and talked to his father in a language he could not understand. Then Ordelerius told his son that he was going to send him far away across the sea to be a monk. Orderic wept to leave his father and mother and the river Severn and the land of England. His father wept, too, as he tied up Orderic's little bundle of clothes and gave him into the care of Rainald.

So Orderic travelled across the sea to Normandy—like Joseph being taken into Egypt, he said. There, at the monastery of S. Evroul, he was given a new name, Vitalis, and began to learn how to be a monk. All round him strange monks spoke a strange language he could not understand, and at first he was very frightened and lonely for he was only ten years old. But soon he learnt the language (Latin) and began to enjoy the new life. He grew up happily and lived sixty years in his monastery, doing a lot of writing in the cloister, except when, in winter-time, his fingers were so numb that he could not write. He wrote history books and loved talking to old knights who visited the monastery about the exciting fights they had had. He never saw his father and mother again, but he never forgot England and the happy life he had lived by the river Severn.

Told by Orderic Vitalis himself.

76

Monks caught feasting

Some monks one day prepared a feast for themselves of tasty meat dishes and choice wine which they dare not eat openly for fear of the Abbot. So they had their feast inside a great wine barrel in the cellarium! Now someone told the Abbot where they were enjoying themselves and so he went and found them. Then they were all afraid, but he pretended to be merry and asked if he could join the feast. They dare not say No, so they all feasted together. But the next day the Abbot got up in chapter and confessed that he had feasted by stealth in the wine barrel, against St. Benedict's Rule. Then he ordered the Prior to punish him by beating. This made the greedy monks ashamed, so they all got up and confessed the same sin and were all well and soundly beaten.

Told by Caesar of Heisterbach.

Here is a picture of another monk caught in the cellarium:

Abbot Samson

There was once a famous Abbot of the Benedictine monastery of Bury St. Edmunds whose name was Samson. One of his monks, Jocelyn of Brakelond, has described him for us:

Abbot Samson was middling tall and almost entirely bald (though what hair he had was black and curly); his face was neither round nor long, his nose big, his lips thick, his eyes clear as crystal and of penetrating glance; his hearing was of the sharpest; his eyebrows grew long and had often to be clipped; a slight cold soon made him hoarse. On the day of his election as Abbot he was forty-seven and had been a monk for seventeen years. He had then a few white hairs in his red beard, but within fourteen years of his election he was white as snow. He was very strong and always ready to travel on horseback or on foot until old age made him less eager. When he heard of the capture of Jerusalem (by Saladin and the Saracens in 1187) he began to wear a hair shirt instead of wool and to give up eating meat. Sweet milk, honey and such sweet things he liked to eat more than any other food. He hated liars, drunkards and wordy fellows. He condemned those who grumbled at their food.

Why do you think Abbot Samson put on a hair shirt and gave up eating meat when he heard of the capture of Jerusalem by the Saracens?

How Abbot Samson saved the monks from fire

One day Abbot Samson was travelling round to see if all the abbey's farms were being properly looked after. At night he was sleeping very soundly in one of the farms when suddenly, in a dream, he heard a voice saying: "Samson, arise quickly!" and again, "Arise, make haste!" Jumping up quickly, he looked around and there was a lighted candle, left carelessly by a monk, which was just going to fall over among the straw on the floor! You know how straw flares up when you put a light to it. Samson was just in time to put out the candle before there was a great blaze. Then he looked all round the house and saw that the doors were so tightly barred and the windows so tightly shut that they would never have escaped in time if the place had really caught fire. So the Abbot and the monks with him gave thanks to God.

Told by Jocelyn of Brakelond.

A Lay Brother's Dream

There was a lay-brother in one of the granges of a Cistercian monastery whose job it was to drive the oxen. He was a man of pure heart and great simplicity who did promptly all he was told to do and toiled daily with great patience. One day he saw in a dream how the Lord Jesus walked with him on the other side of the wagon, bearing in His sweet hand a goad and helping him to drive the oxen. When he awoke and remembered the gentleness and sweetness of his dearly-beloved fellow-worker, his heart was aflame with love.

Told by Caesar of Heisterbach.

Abbot Suger

The great monastery of St. Denis in France once had a great Abbot named Suger. Unlike St. Bernard, Suger wanted to give glory to God by making his abbey as rich and beautiful as possible. So he set to work, first of all, pulling down old walls, rebuilding them and enlarging the church. Then he sent messengers to find the best painters to decorate the church in gold and scarlet and blue. He found bronze workers to make gilded bronze doors on which were shown the Resurrection and Ascension of Christ. For the High Altar he had a golden cloth made (called a frontal) which glistened with rubies, sapphires, emeralds and other precious stones. He persuaded kings and princes to give their jewels and all these decorated the church of St. Denis. On either side of the altar he placed two golden candlesticks given by King Louis of France. In the middle of the choir, with outstretched wings stood a great eagle for a lectern to carry the Bible. All the gold had been rubbed off it, so Abbot Suger had it re-gilded until it shone exceedingly. Also he fetched cunning craftsmen to make brilliant stained-glass windows of sapphire and ruby glass with pictures of Moses and other people from the Bible.

All this building meant a lot of worry and thought for Abbot Suger. He used to lie awake in bed thinking of difficulties, but they always got solved somehow. When they wanted more stone for building, a wonderful new quarry was discovered just at the right moment; when they were short of workmen, a crowd of them suddenly appeared. One day the builders needed very long wooden beams and people shook their heads over this, saying that there were no trees tall enough in the country round.

79

Abbot Suger puzzled over this until he had the idea of going himself to look for tall trees. So, getting up early, he took the right measurements and set off with the carpenters to the forest. The foresters laughed at him, for they knew of no trees tall enough, but Abbot Suger, with the courage of his faith, began pushing his way through thick thorny tangles, and behold! in a short while he had found twelve trees which were tall enough! So they were cut down and used as beams in the church roof to God's glory.

At last the day came to consecrate the new buildings. Many visitors were to be invited and Abbot Suger was worried because food was scarce, especially mutton, since there had lately been a plague among the sheep. He was hurrying through the cloister, wondering where to get food, when a strange monk stopped him. Suger was a little cross, for he was very busy, but the monk said "We hear that you need mutton and so our monastery has sent you a great flock of rams." Then Suger was delighted and said this was the gift of God.

His messengers went out on horseback, north, south, east and west, to all parts of France, calling archbishops, bishops, abbots and noblemen to the consecration of their church. King Louis and Queen Eleanor arrived and a great crowd of nobles, knights and churchmen. All through the night before the great day, the monks prayed in church for God's blessing. In the early morning, bishops and abbots, arrayed in white robes and splendid jewels, with mitres on their heads and *croziers* in their hands, came in solemn procession to bless the church. While they were sprinkling it with holy water, the crowds outside were so huge that the king himself and the nobles had to hold them back. After the consecration, everyone went in splendid procession with crosses and candlesticks round the cloister. "A marvel to behold!" exclaimed Abbot Suger, "Never had anyone seen such a procession!" They ended with the service of High Mass in the church and Suger thought it was a choir of angels that sang *Blessed be the glory of the Lord from His place*.

So Abbot Suger worked and built and made beautiful the house of God. To show his love for it he had some verses written in gold letters on one wall. Here are two lines of his verses:

For the splendour of the church that has fostered and exalted him,
Suger has laboured for the splendour of the church.

Often he used to go in to the church to gaze on the golden altar and cross flashing with brilliant jewels. Then the loveliness of the bright gems would make him forget all his daily business of the monastery, and he would think for a little while that he had been carried away into a heavenly place.

Told by Abbot Suger himself.

The Humble Monk

In a certain monastery there was a rule that at dinner all the crumbs of bread must be gathered together and eaten, so that nothing was wasted. One day all the monks sat eating in silence in the refectory while the Reader read clearly and solemnly from the Bible. A monk, named Odo, was so lost in thought about the words he heard that he forgot to gather up his crumbs. Suddenly the Reader stopped, the bell rang, and all the monks stood up ready to go to the church and give thanks for their meal. Odo came back to himself with a bump, hastily scrambled together his crumbs and ran after the procession clutching them in his hand. When the prayers were over, he knelt humbly before the Abbot and begged pardon. "For what?" said the Abbot. "Because I forgot to eat my crumbs," said Odo, and he held out his handful. But instead of crumbs his hand was full of pearls!

Told by Caesar of Heisterbach.

HOW DO WE KNOW?

The monks of past ages have left us quite a lot of clues for finding out how they lived and what they thought and felt. Here are some of the clues which I have used in writing this book for you. Some of these you can understand for yourselves by using your eyes, but the books in my list are in Latin, so you must learn this language first before you can use these clues for yourselves.

Clues to be found in books

Monastic Rules. Starting from St. Benedict, many heads of monasteries wrote down rules or customs of the monastery and these tell us a great deal about the way they lived.

Monastic Account Books. The various officials of the monastery often kept careful accounts of all they bought and sold. From these we learn about the daily life of the monks. From books called *cartularies* we learn how much land they possessed.

Lives of holy monks written by other monks who knew them. Walter Daniel's life of Ailred told me a great deal about Ailred, and there are many other lives like this.

Books written about the monastic life by monks themselves. There are, for instance, Ailred's own books and many more like them. These show us the monks' thoughts about the hard things and the joyful things in their lives.

Clues to be seen with your own eyes

The remains of monasteries still left today

If you have learnt from this book what the usual plan of a monastery was like, you can probably, when you visit a monastic ruin, trace out for yourself where the different buildings were. But remember, monasteries were not always built on the regular pattern and you may find something peculiar—for example, the dormitory in an unusual place.

Photographs of monasteries from the air

A particularly clever photographer has gone up in an aeroplane especially to get pictures of monasteries from above, and these have been printed in a book you might get from your public library, by Prof. Knowles, called *Monastic Sites from the Air*. You can see the whole pattern of the monasteries very well in these photographs.

Illuminated manuscripts written and painted by the monks themselves

These show us, not only the way the monks wrote, drew and painted, but also many pictures of monks doing all kinds of things in the monastery, for the artists used their eyes and often drew the people around them. Many of the pictures in this book have been taken from those drawn by monks.

Rich treasures of gold, silver and embroidery, etc., which once adorned the monastic churches

Many of these (crucifixes, chalices, altar frontals, mitres, etc.) are now to be seen in our museums. Remember that you will not find many of these rich treasures from *Cistercian* monasteries (I hope you know the reason why), but the *Benedictine* houses especially were very richly decorated.

Here is the beautiful silver chalice which once belonged to Abbot Suger. You can see that it is set with fine jewels.

THINGS TO DO

1. Write a conversation between Ailred and one of his friends at King David's court in which Ailred is explaining why he wants to become a monk at Rievaulx and the friend is trying to stop him.

2. Write an account of what the monks did in each of the following places: the cloister, the parlour, the chapter-house, the dorter, the frater.

3. Make a time-table of the monk's day, drawing pictures to show what they did in each part of the day.

4. Which would you have liked most to be—the Sacrist, the Precentor, the Cellarer, the Kitchener or the Almoner?

5. Paint a picture of the monks at Rievaulx going in procession along the cloister with crosses and lighted candles.

6. Paint a picture of the first monks at Fountains worshipping under the great elm-tree.

7. Make a model of a Cistercian monastery with all the different buildings in the right place.

8. If you have a library or museum near with old manuscripts in it, find out if any of them were written by monks and, if so, from what monastery they came.

9. If there is an ancient monastery, nunnery or friary near you, visit it and see if you can trace out the plan of the buildings. Notice if the plan is the same as that of Rievaulx or different.

10. Write out one of the short psalms (e.g. Psalm 23) as beautifully as you can and try to decorate it, as the monks did, with patterns or pictures. Remember that they liked to make large, elaborate capital letters.

11. Study the two maps on pages 85 and 86. If you live in either of these districts, find out all you can about the monasteries shown on these maps. Otherwise make a similar map of your own district and find out about the monasteries you mark on it.

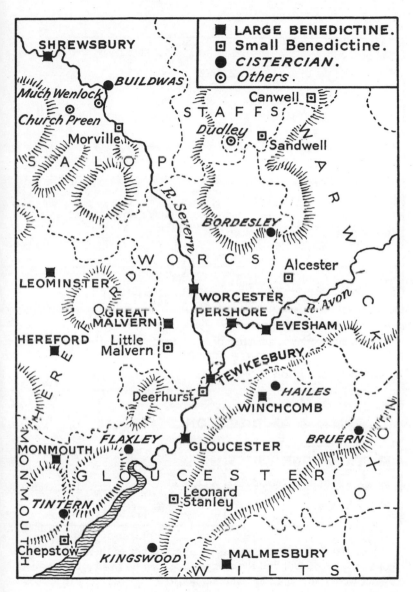

LARGE BENEDICTINE.
Small Benedictine.
CISTERCIAN.
Others.

SHREWSBURY

Much Wenlock BUILDWAS
Church Preen
Morville
SALOP

Canwell
STAFFS
Dudley Sandwell

R. Severn

WORCS

BORDESLEY

Alcester

LEOMINSTER
GREAT MALVERN
HEREFORD
Little Malvern
HEREFORD

WORCESTER
PERSHORE
R. Avon
EVESHAM

TEWKESBURY
Deerhurst
HAILES
WINCHCOMB

FLAXLEY
MONMOUTH
GLOUCESTER
BRUERN

GLOUCESTER

TINTERN
MONMOUTH
Leonard Stanley

OXON

Chepstow
KINGSWOOD
MALMESBURY
WILTS

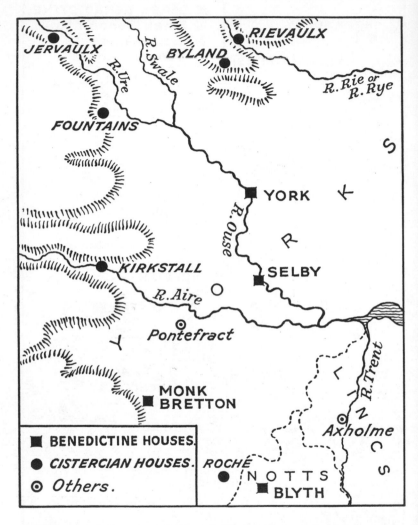

These maps show two districts in England where there were many monasteries. You will find Rievaulx on the map on this page. In which district were there more Benedictine houses?

This map shows the chief places in England and Europe where
monasteries were situated.

GLOSSARY

This is a list of special words. If the word you want to know is not here, look for it in your dictionary.

abbey: home of monks (same as *monastery*).
abbot: head of an abbey or monastery.
almoner: monk who gave food and clothes to poor people.
aumbry: cupboard.
belfry: tower with a bell.
bellows: used for blowing up a fire.
cantor: monk in charge of the singing (same as *precentor*).
carrel: little compartment in the cloister for writing and studying.
cauldron: large iron pot for boiling.
cellarer: monk in charge of the stores.
cellarium: large store-house.
chalice: cup used for Communion.
chapter: meeting of all the monks to settle the business of the monastery.
chapter-house: place where the chapter met.
chronicle: history-book, often written by monks about the history of the monastery.
cloisters: four covered walks built in a square with an open space in the middle.
compline: last service of the day, just before going to bed.
counsellor: someone who gives advice.
cowl: hood worn by monks.
cresset: kind of lamp.
dale: valley.
dorter: dormitory where monks slept.
to excavate: to dig up.
frater: monks' dining-room (same as *refectory*).

grange : small farm.

guest-master : monk who looked after guests.

habit : tunic or gown worn by monks.

illuminator : painter.

infirmarian : monk in charge of the infirmary.

infirmary : hospital for sick and old monks.

kitchener : monk in charge of the cooking.

lauds : service sung by monks at sunrise (same as *matins*).

lectern : reading-desk.

manuscript : book written by hand.

matins : service sung by monks at sunrise (same as *lauds*).

mitre : special cap worn on the head by a bishop or abbot.

mixt : breakfast or light lunch eaten before monks' main meal.

monastery : home of monks (same as *abbey*).

nave : main long part of the church.

nones : fourth service of the day.

novice : someone learning to be a monk.

novice-master . teacher of the novices.

parchment : skin scraped smooth to use for writing books.

parlour : monks' speaking-room.

penance : punishment for wrong-doing.

pot-herbs : vegetables.

pottage : soup.

precentor : monk in charge of the singing (same as *cantor*).

presbytery : end of the church at which the altar stood.

prime : first service of the day.

prior : second in command in the monastery.

psalter : book of Psalms.

pulpitum : screen across the church.

pulse : food made of peas or beans.

refectorian : monk in charge of the refectory.

refectory : monks' dining-room (same as *frater*).

rood-screen : screen across the church.

sacrist : monk in charge of the church.

sacristy : room in which the sacrist kept things for the church.

scapular : piece of cloth worn to hang down back and front.
scribe : writer.
scriptorium : writing-room of a monastery.
sext : third service of the day.
squilla : smallest monastery bell.
stall : wooden seat in the church.
steward : someone who looks after his lord's business.
tallow : fat from which candles are made.
tierce : second service of the day.
transept : part of the church at right angles to the main length.
vespers : fifth service of the day, at dusk.
vestments : special robes worn for church services.
vigils : service sung by monks about 2 a.m. in the night.
vow : very solemn promise.